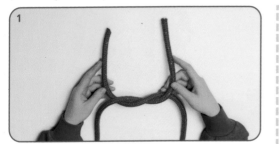

The reef knot is one of the most widely used, but equally most widely misused knots for joining two ropes. **Important:** It should only be used to join lines of equal size and type. The reef knot is reliable as long as tension is applied to both parts. It is easily released by pulling on one of the ends. It is used as a binding knot to bind something or used in reefing a sail. For these reasons it should never be used as a bend (a knot tying the ends of two free lines together).

1 Cross both ends over each other ...

2 ... bring one end forward and cross it over again.

3 The end which was originally on top must when crossed ...

4 ... end up on top again. Pull on all parts.

This bend is used to join two ropes of unequal size. The advantage of this bend is that with increased tension the knot becomes tighter, making it more secure.

1 Make a bight with the thicker of the two ropes to be tied and hold it in one hand. The thinner rope (in the other hand) is passed up through the bight ...

2 ... and once round the back – the direction isn't important. For more security pass it round the bight twice or ...

3 ... three times round the bight, as the increased friction will make it stronger. The thinner rope then passes over ...

4 ... both parts of the bight, down and under itself. Pull on both ends of the rope.

4 Slipped reef knot

This knot is generally used with thinner ropes, such as mainsail reefing lines.

1 Tie an overhand knot ...

2 ... and make a bight with the right end of the rope lying over the overhand knot with the opening to the right.

3 Tie an overhand knot with the left end ...

4 ... and be careful to form a reef knot rather than a granny knot.

5 Fisherman's knot

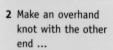

Invented in the nineteenth century, this is also known as the Englishman's, lover's or angler's knot. It is primarily used to join fishing line, twine or thin cord and is a bit bulky. The knot is strong and therefore extremely popular with fishermen.

1 Place both ropes parallel and close to each other. Make an overhand knot with one end around the other rope.

2 Make an overhand knot with the other end ...

3 ... over the first.

4 Pull on both working ends, until the knots make contact with each other. The knots should now be next to each other.

The sheet bend is one of a few knots that can successfully tie together two ropes of different thickness and structure. It can also be used to join flag halyards to the corners of a flag. The knot becomes tighter as it is subjected to greater strain.

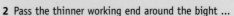

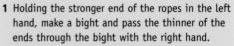

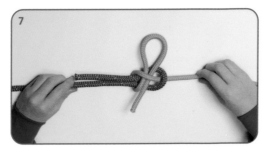

1. Holding the stronger end of the ropes in the left hand, make a bight and pass the thinner of the ends through the bight with the right hand.

2. Pass the thinner working end around the bight ...

3. ... and pass the end ...

4. ... underneath itself and through.

5. The slipped sheet bend is easier to untie when the rope is under strain.

6. The slipped version is formed by making a bight with the thinner end ...

7. ... and then looping it back through the tuck.

8. The double sheet bend is even stronger and is made by bringing the working end around twice (or possibly more times) ...

9. ... round the thicker bight and each time through the tuck.

This knot is named after Dr Edward Hunter who in 1978 was credited with its invention. Dr Hunter had used it for years to tie broken shoelaces, and it is certainly very secure, whilst being easy to untie. The Hunter's bend is used in a similar way to a sheet bend but the result is bulkier.

1 Make a large, loose, overhand knot, keeping it vertical.

2. Pass the end of the second rope from behind and up through the lower loop and behind its own standing part.

3. Tuck the end from behind again, through the top loop and again underneath and through itself.

4. Pull vertically on both standing parts ...

5. ...and the knot becomes tight and secure.

8 Carrick bend

This knot is formed by two loops entwined in one another. The carrick bend offers a safe way of joining two ropes of similar diameter but different materials. It's not very useful at sea because it is difficult to untie, but it is used in anchoring and mountain climbing to join heavy ropes together.

1 Make a loop, with the working end behind its own standing part.

2 Make a loop with the other end as follows: lay it under the first loop, pass over the standing part and under the working end from above and through the first loop ...

3 ... then continue under its own standing part and over the working end ...

4 ... of the first loop, away and out.

5 Pull equally on the two standing ends ...

6 ...to tighten the knot.

This hitch is used to secure one line to another fixed line or spar, for example a tow rope, or to secure a line to a sheet where the load has to be reduced. The working line should be thinner than the fixed line.

1 Make a loop around the hawser with the working end away from you, and then behind the standing part of the line.

2 Make a turn around the hawser ...

3 ... between the first loop and the standing part.

4 Make another turn in front of the already-made hitch, by tucking the working end up and through.

5 The hitch can be moved along the fixed line when tension is released and ...

6 ... will tighten itself again where load is applied.

10 Racking bend (heaving line bend)

When a heaving line has to be attached to a mooring, towing or other rope, you need a knot that is easy to tie, that is safe and – equally important – easy to untie. This one isn't pretty, but it does the job.

1 Use the thicker of the lines to make a bight and, with the working end of the thinner line, make an overhand loop over the standing part of the thicker.

2 Pass the working end over and through the bight of the thicker line.

3 Lay the working end over again and through the bight.

4 Repeat this racking/weaving process as many times as necessary.

5 To finish it off, pass the working end between the last two racking turns to the front of the large bight.

6 Pull on the working and standing ends to tighten and secure the knot.

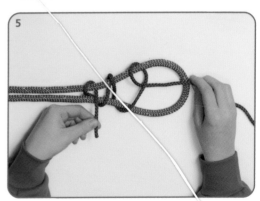

11 Round turn and two half hitches

To secure lines onto thin beams, this hitch is more suitable than the clove hitch, which can become too tight.

1 Make one and a half turns around the beam, finishing with both ends running alongside each other.

2 Tie a half turn around the standing part ...

3 & 4 ... and in the same direction tie a second half turn.

5 Pull on the standing end to tighten.

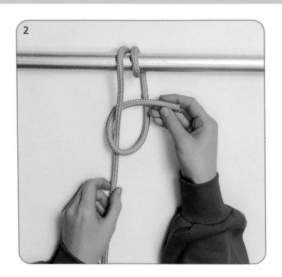

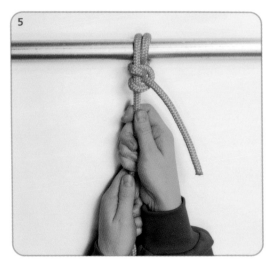

To tie a fender to a guardrail is the easiest thing in the world: a quick clove hitch or a round turn and two half hitches on the wire, and the fender is secure. Both methods have one disadvantage: the hitch can become very tight and difficult to untie with cold and wet hands. Using a highwayman's hitch can overcome this problem. The highwayman's hitch is totally secure, but a quick tug on the end rope will easily release it. The hitch then falls like magic from the wire.

1. Make a bight with the fender rope on the outside of the guardrail, pulling against the wire.

2. Pass a bight of the fender line under and through ...

3. ... and make a second bight through the first.

4. Then with the working end under the wire make a further bight.

5. Pull on the fender rope – finished. To release, pull on the working end.

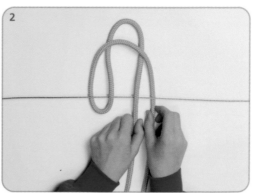

The clove hitch is the best choice when a rope needs to be tied to a bollard or boom. With one end of the object open, the hitch can be tied and dropped over it, the advantage being that the whole rope doesn't have to be pulled through. The often forgotten use for the clove hitch is to retrieve items that have gone overboard.

1 If a clove hitch is to be made around a post ...

2 ... make two overhand loops, place them ...

3 ...on top of one another ...

4 & 5 ... and over the post.

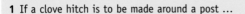

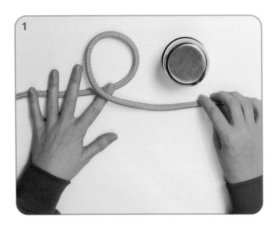

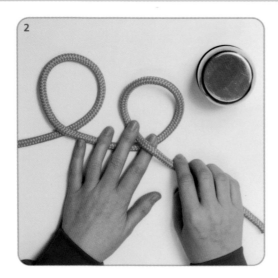

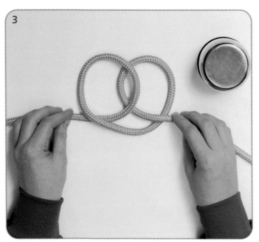

The clove hitch tied with a working end is used on objects where there is no free end to place the hitch over, for example a rail. This variation has the disadvantage that the whole rope has to be pulled through.

1 Place the working end over the boom, then bring it from behind and around the standing part.

2 Pass it forward and over the boom again ...

3 ... and under and through the standing part.

4 & 5 Pull both parts close to one another.

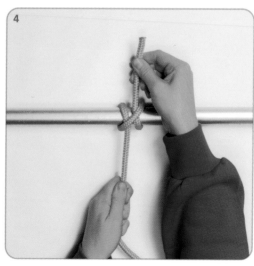

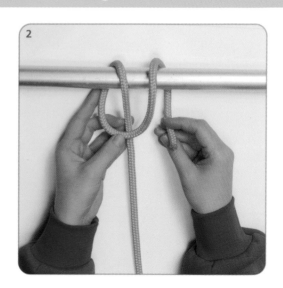

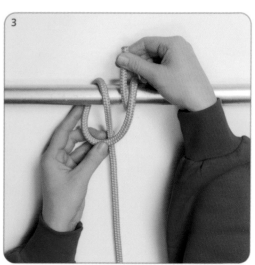

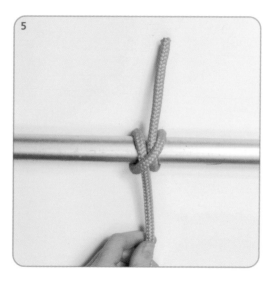

Tying a bowline is relatively easy but the method is often quickly forgotten. A helpful saying is: 'The rabbit comes out of the hole, goes round the tree and back down the hole.' The rabbit is the rope, the hole is the loop and the tree is the standing end.

The bowline is one of the most important knots and has all the characteristics one expects of a good knot. It is absolutely secure, doesn't slip and is easy to untie, even under tension.

1 Make a loop (with the end lying on top) and hold it tight.

2 With the other hand, pass the working end from underneath through the loop ...

3 ... and around the rope. The direction in which the working end gets passed around the rope has no effect whatsoever on the strength of the final knot.

4 The working end passes through the loop again from the top to complete the knot.

5 Now start to tighten the bowline, ensuring that the main loop is of the required size.

6 Tighten the knot and it's ready for use.

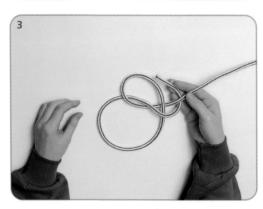

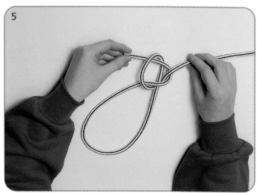

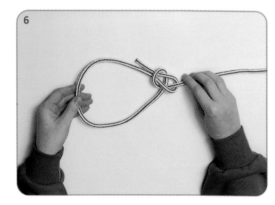

The bowline is without doubt one of the most secure knots you can use to attach ropes to an object. Onboard, before mooring, a bowline can be tied in the end of a rope so that the loop can be easily placed over a bollard or cleat. But what happens if there is only a ring on the pontoon and the skipper insists on a bowline? The steps below show what to do in exactly this situation. Steps 1 and 2 can be prepared on board and held in one hand, so only the bight is open. The end is then passed through the ring, after which nothing can go wrong!

1. Make a loop in the loose end of the rope and a bight with the standing end ...

2. ... passing under and through the loop. Hold the knot so that the bight is open.

3. Pass the loose end through the tying ring on the pontoon and through the bight.

4. The loose end, together with the two ends which have been passed through the ring, should be ...

5. ... held tightly.

6. The bowline tightens with load on the standing end.

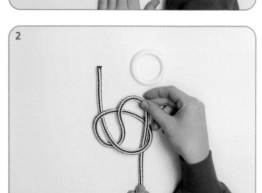

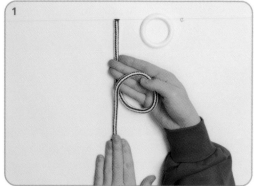

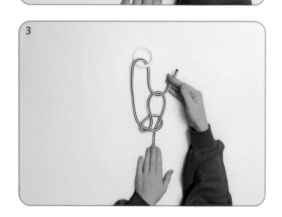

The bowline on the bight is made from two secure loops, running parallel, but they can be used separately. It is a very old knot, and is mainly used in sea rescue. If the person to be rescued is conscious, they place one leg in one loop, the other leg in the second loop and he/she holds on to the standing end. If the person is unconscious, then both legs are put through one loop, and the second loop is placed around the chest and under the arms. In addition to this, the bowline on the bight is a safe method for recovering objects lost overboard.

1 Make a bight in the rope.

2 Form a loop ...

3 ... and put the bight through the loop.

4 Open the bight downwards, passing around the loop and behind the standing part.

5 Pull equally on the standing ends and both loops.

18 Portuguese bowline

Portuguese sailors used this knot (or hitch) in bygone days to lay out an anchor. It is also known as a 'caulking bowline' because caulkers used it to suspend themselves while working on boats – they placed the first loop around their backs, and sat in the second loop. The Portuguese bowline is useful to strengthen the hold on an object, especially when it is very heavy. It can be tied with two or more loops: the more loops, the stronger the knot.

1 & 2 Form a loop in the standing part, pass the end through the object and then through the previously made loop.

3 Pass the working end under the standing part and form a second loop around the object.

4 Pass the working end through the loop of the standing part ...

5 ... carry it round again, but in the opposite direction through its loop.

6 To tighten the knot, hold onto the loop and pull on the standing end.

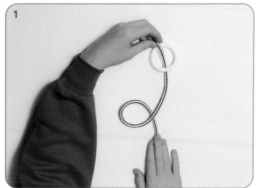

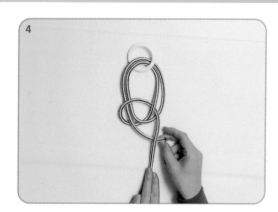

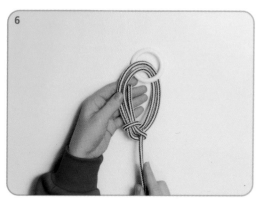

This ancient knot (or hitch) is known to sailors as the Spanish bowline. It is used in different situations, including rescues at sea and to lift objects in a horizontal position. It is made out of two separate loops which have a tight hold and are secure, even under heavy strain: the knot can even take the weight of scaffolding if the rigging is strong enough.

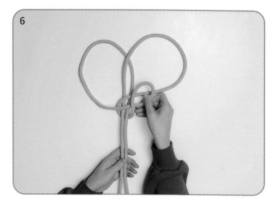

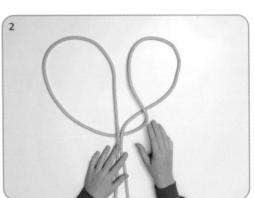

1 Form two big loops.

2 Twist the right loop round to the left ...

3 ... and the left one round to the right.

4 Pass the left loop from underneath up through the right ...

5 ... forming a third loop.

6 With the right hand, pull this third loop out to the right, twist it and pass it through the upper right-handed loop.

7 & 8 Repeat this on the left side and pass the newly made loop through the upper left-hand loop.

9 Bring both newly made loops together ...

10 ... and hold with the left thumb.

11 Pull on the two parallel standing ends to tighten.

12 The finished bowline has two outward facing loops.

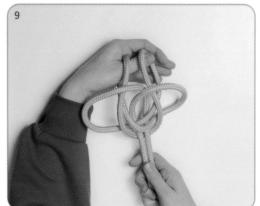

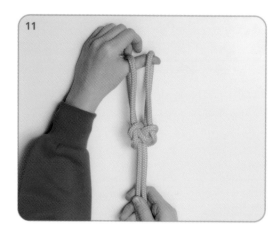

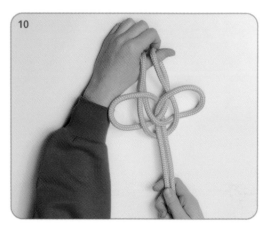

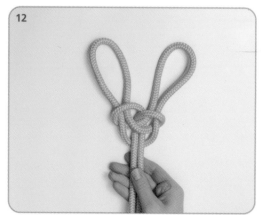

The anchor bend is commonly used to tie a chain to an anchor. Instead of two half turns at the end, you can also use a bowline.

1 Pass the working end twice through the ring ...

2 ... around the standing end and through the two turns on the ring.

3 Then finish ...

4 ... the working end with ...

5 ... a half hitch ...

6 ... to secure it.

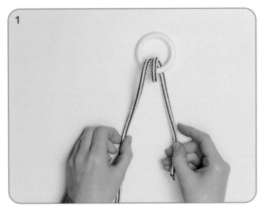

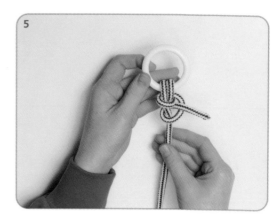

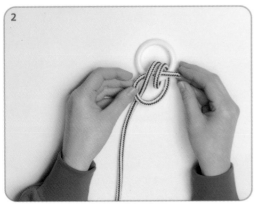

Don't forget that synthetic fibres swell when they become wet and sheets always need to be ready for quick release.

1 Make a turn around the cleat, so that the line doesn't kink.

2 Then make a few figure of eight turns around the horns on the cleat ...

3 & 4 ... so that the line is held securely.

5 If the line isn't held securely, twist the loose end of the rope 180° on the last diagonal turn and make a locking turn on the horn. The working end should run parallel to the second to last diagonal turn. A sheet should never be locked in this way.

6 Instead of the locking turn, secure it with a slipped sheet bend, with the sheet in the form of a bight under the last diagonal turn, which is pulled up and through.

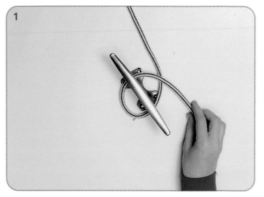

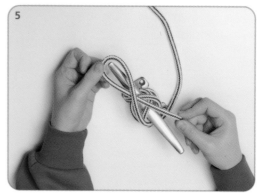

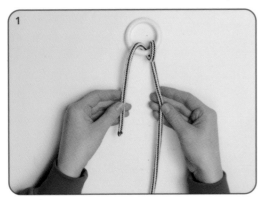

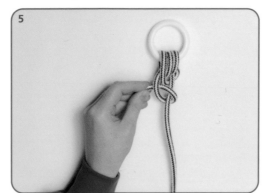

This hitch, used by sailors to tie a rope to an anchor, is also known as the double anchor bend. It is even more secure than the normal anchor bend, but is generally only used with ropes of a small to middle size diameter, because it is difficult to tie with thicker rope.

1 Pass the working end through the ring ...

2 ... and make two or three round turns, without twisting it.

3 Pass the working end behind the standing part ...

4 ... and through the round turns.

5 & 6 The hitch is finished, but for more security, one or two half hitches can be tied and tightened separately. If the ring, in relation to the rope, is too thin then three or four half hitches can be tied.

23 Buntline hitch

The buntline hitch is used to fix ropes or lines to eyes or onto sails. The advantage of this knot is its compactness, allowing a halyard shackle to be pulled up close to the masthead to give a tighter luff. The buntline hitch tightens itself under a heavy load and a marlin spike is usually required to release it.

1 Pass the working end down and through the shackle, taking it under and round the standing part.

2 Make a round turn. Pass the working end once around the newly formed loop ...

3 ... and pass it from left to right through the loop, with the working end going out over the standing part ...

4 ... and under and through the round turn.

5 Pull the knot tightly.

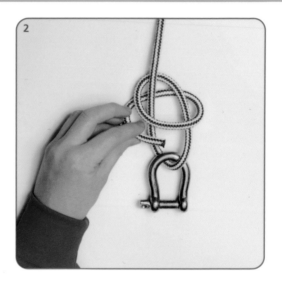

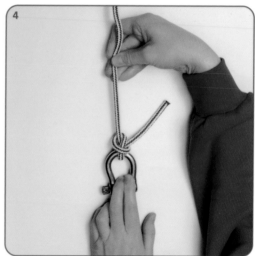

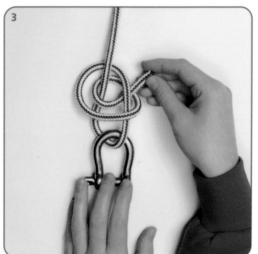

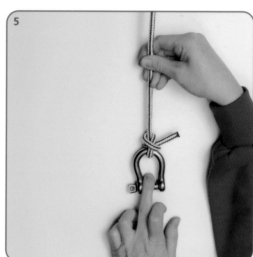

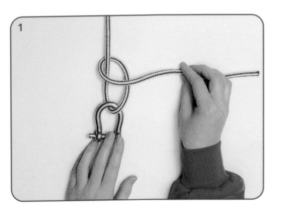

With this knot, you form a loop that can be tightened around an object, and even with repeated pulling it won't loosen up. The knot can be used to secure a line to a harness, bosun's chair, a lifejacket, or shackle – anything you might come up with!

1 Make a loop and pass the working end over and under the loop, forming a figure of eight.

2 Take the free end over the loop.

3 Pass the end through the figure of eight ...

4 ... alongside the standing part.

5 This enables a shackle, for example, to be easily slipped on; just pull the standing end to tighten.

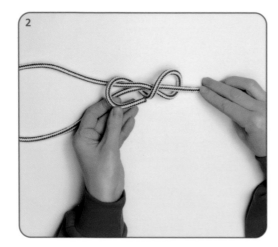

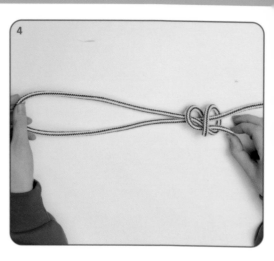

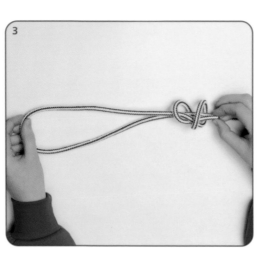

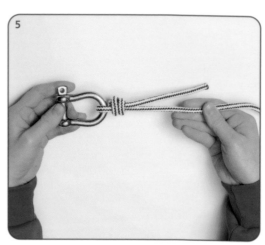

25 Block hitch

This is a special knot that doesn't usually appear in a nautical context, but in isolated cases it can be extremely useful. It makes sense to use it where the knot needs to be closely bound to its object, for example on the lifelines or in the rigging. The friction within the knot is so good that even elastic stays in place.

1 Make a loop and pass the rope through to tie an overhand knot.

2 Take the working end and make a loop by passing it under the rope and up through the loop ...

3 ... to form a second overhand knot.

4 Hold the object and pull the end of the rope ...

5 ... until both knots tighten into one another.

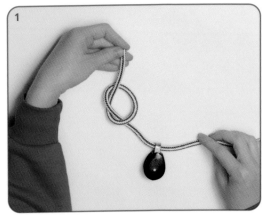

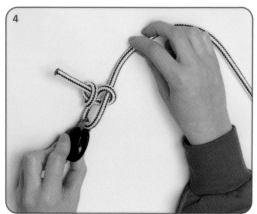

26 Draw loop with a bowline

As the name suggests, two knots form this bowline. It is a good method of fastening a line round a pole and, as with every bowline, it is completely secure. The difference between this and other hitches, for example a clove hitch, is that the draw loop doesn't tighten permanently and can therefore be moved around when the tension is released from the rope.

1 Pass the working end under and around the pole, then once again under and up on top of the boom.

2 The working end needs to be long enough to enable the second knot to be tied around the standing part.

3 This bowline should be big enough ...

4 ... to loosely slide up and down, because ...

5 ... only then will it ensure security by tightening under strain, but open up easily and slide along when not.

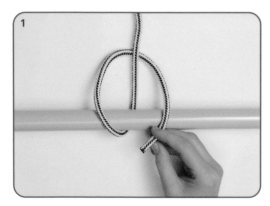

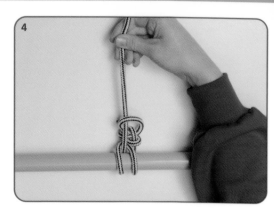

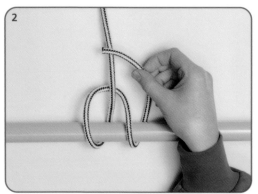

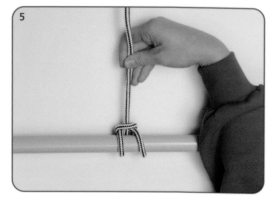

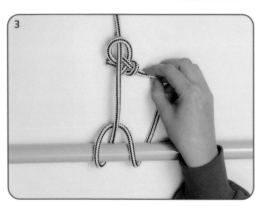

The studdingsail halyard bend is used for tying objects onto a spar or boom. It is more secure than a clove hitch, and has the advantage that when thinner cord is used it is easier to untie. Using this bend, a boom can be tied directly to the block, as there is no space between the knot and the boom.

1 One and a half round turns and ...

2 ... take the working end behind the standing part and place through the round turns.

3 The working end then goes in the opposite direction, over the second round turn ...

4 ... then under and through the first round turn.

5 Holding it in one hand, lead the working end out with the other hand.

6 Pull tightly on both parts.

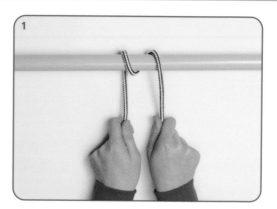

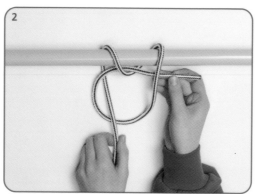

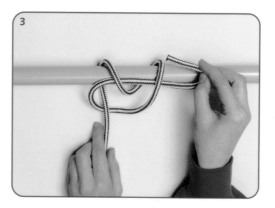

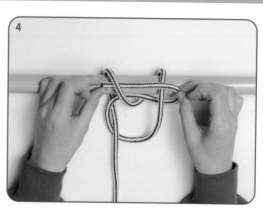

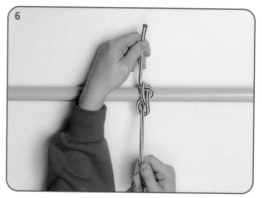

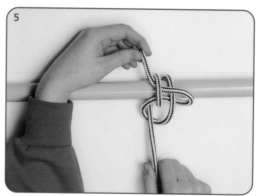

The real name for this knot is a 'hitch for a high pole, pillar or post' – hence the necessity for the shortened version! This knot is hardly pretty but is always reliable and easy to untie, even when hidden beneath a high tide.

1 Double the end of the rope up, and make a round turn with the bight around the pole and under both parts of the standing part.

2 Opening the bight, make another bight with part of the rope and pass it ...

3 ... up and through the first bight, under the round turn ...

4 ... and out through the bight.

5 With tension on the second part, the hitch tightens.

6 By pulling on the loose end, which formed the last bight, it unties.

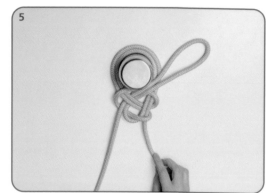

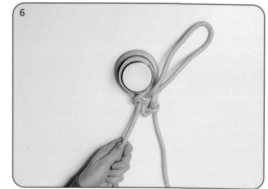

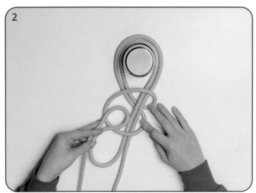

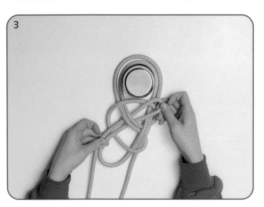

This hitch is especially useful when tying thin cord to heavy weights (such as timber, logs and planks) in order to hoist them. For this reason it is also known as a carpenter's hitch. The knot is easy to untie even after being under extreme tension.

1 Place the cord end around the object and around its own standing part.

2 Turn the end at least twice around the standing part.

3 With round logs use at least 3 turns, covering at least half the width of the timber.

4 Pull tightly.

5 The loop must be pressed firmly against the timber.

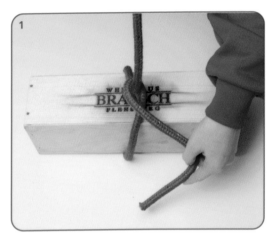

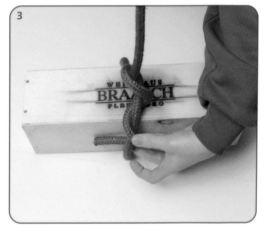

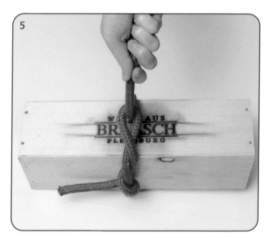

30 Plank sling

Used to make a platform or hanging plank, which you can stand on to do jobs.

1 Make a loop in the rope, making sure the length of the loop is wider than the plank.

2 Make a bight on the outside of the loop by taking it from inside underneath and over the loop.

3 Slide this bight over the plank, with the original loop lying under the plank for support. NB, a piece of wood nailed onto the underside of the plank, right at the end beyond the sling, will prevent the plank being pulled out of the sling.

31 Blackwall hitch

This knot uses a strong rope and is useful if the knot needs to be tied and untied quickly. Be aware that this knot is only secure under a constant load.

1 Lay the end of the rope around the inside of the hook ...

2 ... pass it around the hook and through itself, making a half hitch.

3 Pull on the standing end to tighten.

32 Catspaw

The catspaw is used to attach a hook to a heavy load.

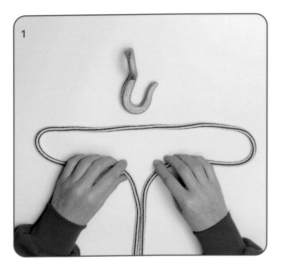

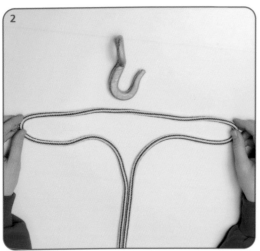

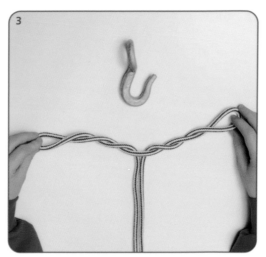

1 Make a bight and press it flat, in the shape of a T.

2 Holding both ends of the loop ...

3 ... twist them 3-4 times in the same direction.

4 Place the twisted loops onto the hook.

5 Pull to tighten.

33 Barrel sling

The barrel sling is used for attaching a rope to a bucket or barrel etc. To ensure that it doesn't slip, two overhand knots are made around the largest part of the container, making a double clove hitch, which supports it and is secure.

1 Place the container on top of the middle of the rope. Tie an overhand knot ...

2 ... and on both sides, pull it apart and place it round the top part of the container.

3 Pull on both parts to tighten and hold the container.

4 As long as there is pressure on the hitch, it will remain secure.

5 To secure it without pressure, tie another overhand knot, thereby tying a double clove hitch.

The figure-of-eight is one of the most commonly used stopper knots, and every sailor learns it early on. Its name represents the shape of the tied knot and it is used as a stopper at the end of a rope, for example on halyards, reefing lines, sheets and kicking straps, to prevent them running through blocks or fairleads. The figure-of-eight is a secure knot and it's relatively easy to undo. It is the foundation for many other knots.

1 Make a bight at the end of the rope ...

2 ... and make half a twist.

3 Pull the working end through the loop ...

4 & 5 ... and pull strongly on both parts to tighten.

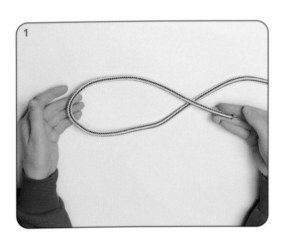

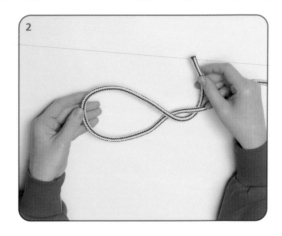

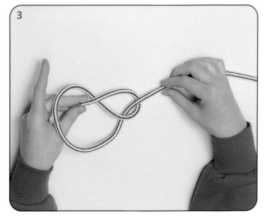

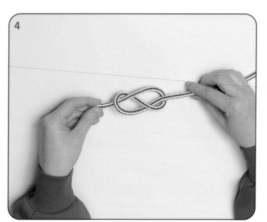

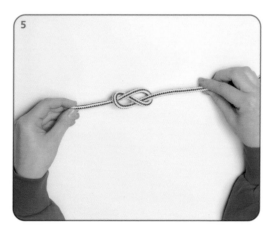

35 Stevedore´s knot

The stevedore's knot is used to secure the end of a cargo tie and prevent it from coming free. It is a continuation of the figure-of-eight knot and is equally easy to untie, but with time it can become ugly and deformed.

1 Make a bight in the end of the line and pass the working end ...

2 ... twice around the standing end.

3 Pass the working end up ...

4 ... and through the loop.

5 & 6 Pull equally on both parts.

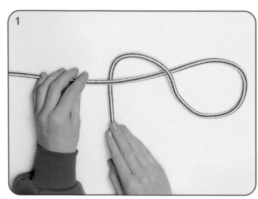

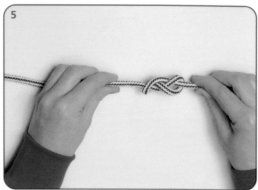

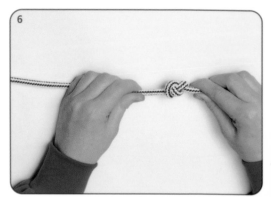

The secret of the heaving line knot lies in its weight. The weight enables the line to be thrown further, pulling the rest of the line behind it. Any rope can be used to tie this knot. In addition, the heaving line knot can be used as a good stopper knot, for example on a dog lead, to prevent it slipping from your hand. Apart from this the knot can also be used on sailors' clothing and sail bags. This knot is easily made and untied.

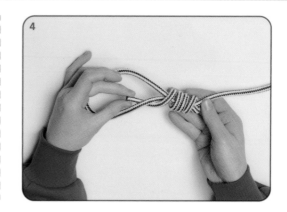

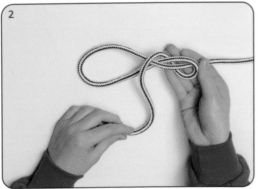

1 Make a long loop ...

2 ... and by passing the working end over and under the standing part ...

3 ... make a lot of turns and leave a long end. The more turns lying next to one another, the heavier and tighter the knot becomes.

4 Pull the end through the rest of the loop ...

5 ... and pull out of the turns.

6 To finish off the knot, pull the rope back out of the knot so that it tightens in itself.

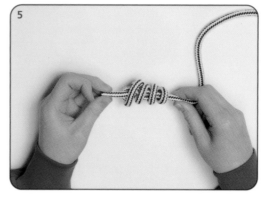

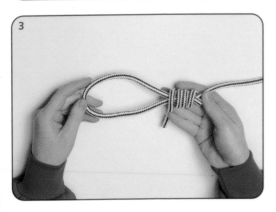

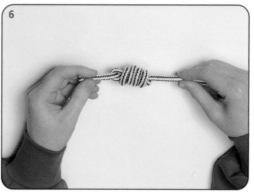

If a loop is needed in the middle of a rope, but it mustn't become smaller when pressure is placed on both parts, then the alpine butterfly is the perfect answer.

1 Make three turns around your hand.

2 Cross the left rope over the one on the right.

3 Pull the new left one over to the right ...

4 ... and tuck it back through.

5 Remove your hand and hold onto the tucked-through loop.

6 Pull on both ends to tighten. An attractive and secure knot, which is so easy to tie!

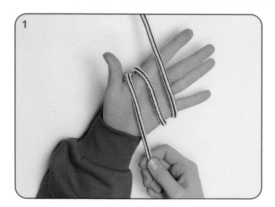

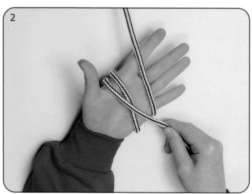

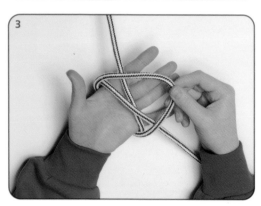

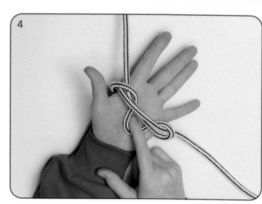

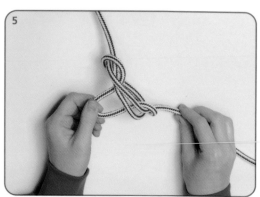

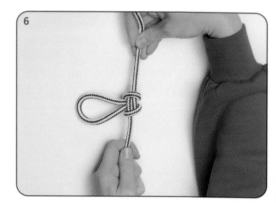

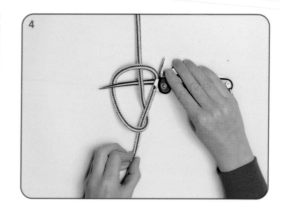

Using a marlin spike hitch with a spike or bar as a handle, this knot provides good pulling grip on a rope. The bar can be held with both hands and the line can be pulled through with more force. The procedure isn't dangerous, because if the pressure on the rope is too strong you can just let go. The spike or bar might escape, but you are guaranteed to keep your fingers!

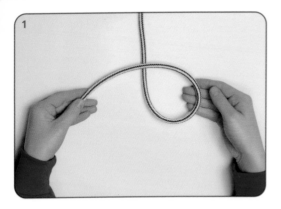

1 Make a loop at the working end of the rope. Take the loop round to the front, place upon the standing end and ...

2 & 3 ... pull the standing part up and out of the loop.

4 Slip the spike or bar under this newly made bight ...

5 ... and pull hard – towards the loose end of the rope. With this grip the line can be pulled strongly.

6 The resulting knot is very strong but can be released with a sharp tug on the end once the spike or bar is removed.

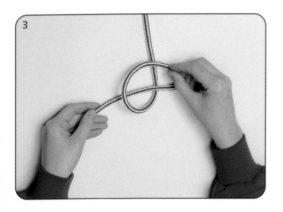

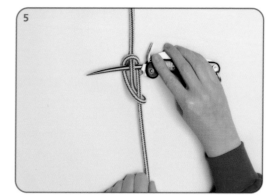

This shortening knot can be used to shorten an end on which there is tension. Without tension, it will fall apart.

1 Make a loop in one end and twist the end underneath into two bights, shaped like an S.

2 Pass the loop of the closest bight into the first loop, ie over the working end of the top part and under the standing part of the loop (half hitch).

3 Make a loop with the end of the part hanging down.

4 & 5 Tie another half hitch ...

6 ... and pull them both tight.

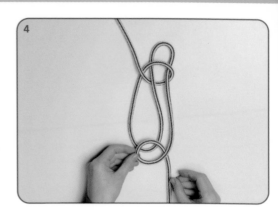

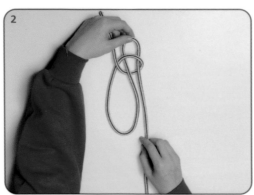

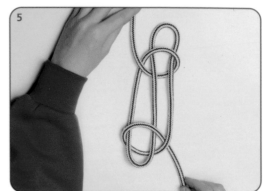

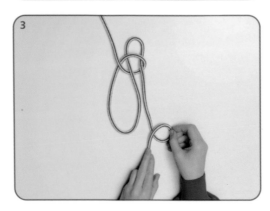

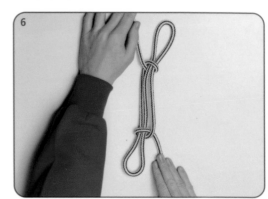